When I Feel
NERVOUS

Amy Beattie

Published in 2020 by Enslow Publishing, LLC
101 W. 23rd Street, Suite 240, New York, NY 10011

Copyright © 2020 by Enslow Publishing, LLC.

All rights reserved.

No part of this book may be reproduced by any means without the written permission of the publisher.

Library of Congress Cataloging-in-Publication Data

Names: Beattie, Amy, author.
Title: When I feel nervous / Amy Beattie.
Description: New York : Enslow Publishing, 2020. | Series: My feelings | Includes bibliographical references and index. | Audience: Grades K-2.
Identifiers: LCCN 2019007732| ISBN 9781978511668 (library bound) | ISBN 9781978511637 (pbk.) | ISBN 9781978511644 (6 pack)
Subjects: LCSH: Anxiety in children—Juvenile literature. | Anxiety—Juvenile literature.
Classification: LCC BF723.A5 B43 2020 | DDC 155.4/1246—dc23
LC record available at https://lccn.loc.gov/2019007732

Printed in the United States of America

To Our Readers: We have done our best to make sure all websites in this book were active and appropriate when we went to press. However, the author and the publisher have no control over and assume no liability for the material available on those websites or on any websites they may link to. Any comments or suggestions can be sent by email to customerservice@enslow.com.

Photo Credits: Cover Tiffany Bryant/Shutterstock.com; cover, p. 1 (emoji) Cosmic_Design/Shutterstock.com; pp. 4, 6, 7 Creatista/Shutterstock.com; p. 5 Flamingo Images/Shutterstock.com; pp. 8, 9 altanaka/Shutterstock.com; pp. 10, 13 EvgeniiAnd/Shutterstock.com; p. 11 Pavel L Photo and Video/Shutterstock.com; p. 12 olsima/Shutterstock.com; pp. 14, 15 Pair Srinrat/Shutterstock.com; pp. 16, 17 JGI/Tom Grill/Getty Images; pp. 18, 20, 21 fizkes/iStock/Getty Images; p. 19 Africa Studio/Shutterstock.com; pp. 22, 23 KatarzynaBialasiewicz/iStock/Getty Images.

Contents

Dance Class 4

Meeting New People 8

Way Up High 10

Haircut 14

Adding Numbers 16

Mom's Job 18

Being Nervous 22

Words to Know 24

Index 24

I feel nervous when I go to a new dance class.

I do not know the other kids. What if they are better dancers than I am?

The teacher puts us into pairs. She asks my partner to show me what to do.

My partner helps me. We work together to learn the steps.

I feel nervous when I meet new people. I hide behind my dad.

My dad tells me their names. They wave.
They say hi to me. I wave back.

I feel nervous when I am up high.

What if I fall? My stomach hurts when I think about it.

I watch my friend take his turn. He holds the ropes. He is so brave.

I can do it, too! I made it to the other side. But I still like playing on the ground better.

I feel nervous when I get a haircut. The scissors are so close to my head!

But the **barber** is very careful. Now my hair looks great!

I feel nervous in math class. Adding big numbers is hard.

My teacher says practice makes perfect.
I decide to keep working.

I feel nervous when my mom loses her job.

What if she cannot find a new job? What if the new job is far away? Then we will have to move.

My mom does not know when she will get a new job. It is hard not to know what will happen!

I wish I could help. But she says she will work hard to find a new job. We all have to be **patient**.

Being nervous is normal when things are new or different. Everyone gets nervous sometimes.

If we help each other, we can get used to new things.

Words to Know

barber Someone who cuts people's hair.

patient Able to wait without getting scared or nervous.

Index

brave, 12
careful, 15
dad, 8, 9
dance, 4–5
friend, 12
haircut, 14–15
help, 23
job, 18–21

math, 16
mom, 18, 20
move, 19
numbers, 16
partner, 6–7
patient, 21
playing, 13
practice, 17

ropes, 12
scissors, 14
stomach, 11
teacher, 6, 17
wave, 9